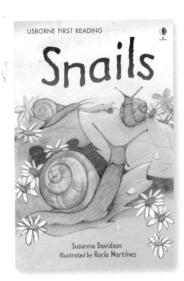

USBORNE FIRST READING

Snails

Susanna Davidson
Illustrated by Rocío Martínez

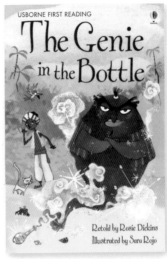

USBORNE FIRST READING

The Genie in the Bottle

Retold by Rosie Dickins
Illustrated by Sara Rojo

USBORNE FIRST READING

THE STONECUTTER

RETOLD BY LYNNE BENTON
ILLUSTRATED BY LEE COSGROVE

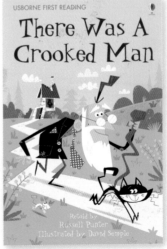

USBORNE FIRST READING

There Was A Crooked Man

Retold by
Russell Punter
Illustrated by David Semple

Bears

Sarah Courtauld

Illustrated by
Masumi Furukawa

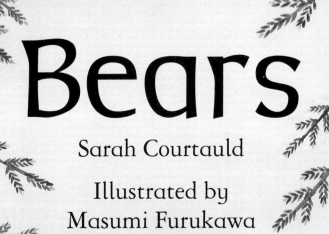

Reading consultant: Alison Kelly
Roehampton University

A big brown
bear is walking
in a forest.

3

She stands up.

She climbs a tree using
her long, sharp claws.

Then she sniffs out
juicy berries to eat.

5

Bears have thick,
heavy coats and
big, furry paws.

Some bears go to rivers
to catch fish.

Panda bears live high
up on cold mountains.

They munch on tough
grass called bamboo.

Polar bears live in the icy Arctic.

Their thick, hairy coats
keep them warm.

11

Each year, bears find
a partner.

Then the female bear digs a den.

She gives birth to baby bears inside the warm, snug den.

They are called cubs.

And they are as
small as apples.

At first, they
can't see or hear.

15

The cubs cuddle up
close to their mother.

She feeds them with
her milk.

Now it is winter.

They all stay curled up
inside the den.

At last, it's spring.
They climb out
into the sun.

The cubs start to play.

They climb
trees.

They fight.

They lick each other's noses. This shows they are friends.

Their mother is
close. She keeps
them safe.

Where bears live

There are eight different kinds of bears. They live all over the world.

Polar bears live in the Arctic.

North America

American black bears live in America.

Brown bears live in North America and Asia.

Spectacled bears live in South America.

South America

South Pacific Ocean

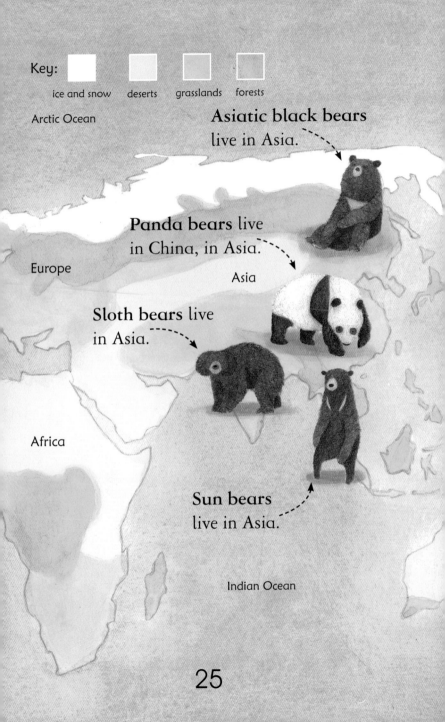

Key: ice and snow deserts grasslands forests

Arctic Ocean

Asiatic black bears live in Asia.

Panda bears live in China, in Asia.

Europe

Asia

Sloth bears live in Asia.

Africa

Sun bears live in Asia.

Indian Ocean

25

Puzzles

Puzzle 1
Match the bear to the place.

Polar bear

Panda bear

Brown bear

A

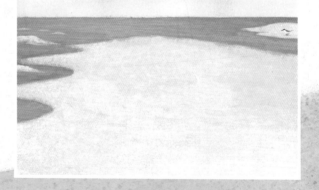

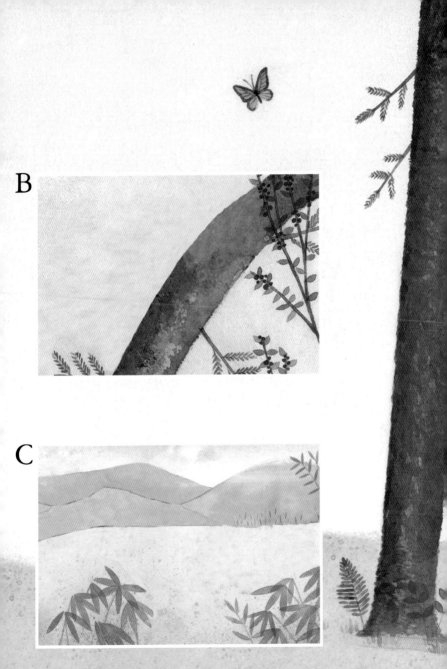

B

C

27

Puzzle 2
Which order should the pictures be in?

A

B

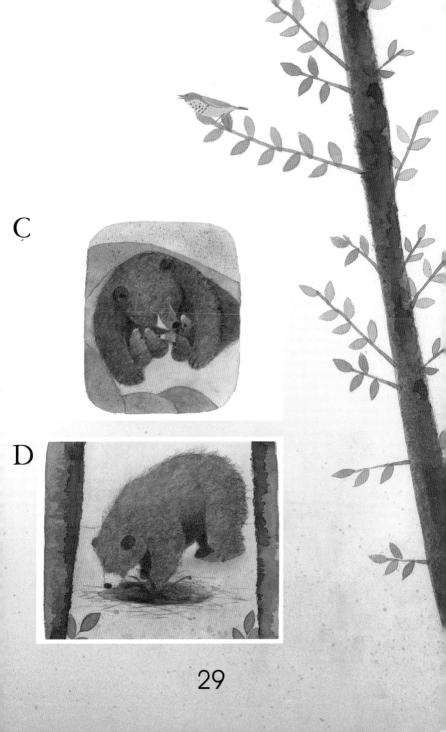

C

D

29

Answers to puzzles

Puzzle 1

A

Polar bear

B

Brown bear

C

Panda bear

Puzzle 2

D

1

C

2

A

3

B

4

Index

Bear websites

For links to websites where you can find out more about bears, go to **www.usborne-quicklinks.com** and type the keywords "first reading bears". Please ask an adult before using the internet.

Internet Guidelines

The recommended websites are regularly reviewed and updated but, please note, Usborne Publishing is not responsible for the content of any website other than its own. We recommend that young children are supervised while on the internet.

Consultant: Mark Brayshaw
Produced in consultation with the
Durrell Wildlife Trust
Designed by Emily Bornoff
Series editor: Lesley Sims
Series designer: Russell Punter

First published in 2010 by Usborne Publishing Ltd., Usborne House, 83-85 Saffron Hill, London EC1N 8RT, England. www.usborne.com
Copyright © 2010 Usborne Publishing Ltd.

USBORNE FIRST READING
Level Three

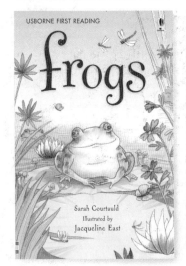